Copyright © 2021 Tekkan
Artwork Copyright © 2021

All rights reserved.
First Printing, 2021
ISBN 978-1-7363537-3-8

To contact Tekkan please email:
buddhaboy1289@gmail.com

I'd like to say thank you to River Maria Urke for her inspired artistry which she uses to encourage me to do my best — may my dedication of this book to her express my gratitude.

How to Read My Poems

I want to be direct in my meaning — I want people to clearly understand my meaning. My wordiness is inspired by Shakespeare, and the (aimed-for) concision is in imitation of Japanese style. Using the sonnet with the tanka, I mix the sensibility of the Occident and the Orient — which I have done by living in England, Japan, and America.

I have married the sonnet to the tanka. Often, I don't rhyme my sonnets, because I want freer expression. I tell a story in the sonnet — using three quatrains separated by line spaces, and a final couplet. The story builds to a conclusion in the couplet. The tanka is a commentary, or a counterpoint, to the sonnet — the combined poems have two endings.

Recently I have added limericks, doggerel, and rhymed sonnets into my repertoire. The limericks have a rhyme scheme but the tanka do not.

I don't punctuate much in my poetry. I want the words themselves to do the work. There is logic between words, and the forms provide structure. By not using punctuation I hope to direct readers to carefully attend to each word — to appreciate the graininess of words.

Reading my poems silently and reading them
Aloud may be different experiences. The way
I've written there's not always a pause
intended at the end of the line.

Hint: *My poems are to be recited not as lines but as
phrases, and a phrase often overflows the break at the end
of a line. I pause and take a breath where it seems natural
for me to pause. Another person may pause differently
than I do.*

Each poem is a piece of a mosaic, and it is
my hope that the collection of poems forms
an accurate portrait of consciousness.

My friend, *Will Ersland*, is a wonderful artist.
His artwork graces this book.

I am Barry MacDonald. I received the *dharma*
name *Tekkan*, which means "Iron Man," a
settled practitioner of great determination.

— *Tekkan*

Everyday Mind XXI

I close my eyes
and the bright sun
turns my eyelids
red.

I sure wouldn't want to live without friends
Because easy conversation is fun
We can find things to do on the weekends
So life is joyous over the long run
But I have to watch my expectations
I need to practice giving and taking
I have to show my appreciation
Can't be the one that's always receiving
It is better to have two points of view
To have a lively and friendly debate
And maybe more or less both views are true
There's a confusing world to celebrate
To keep a friend I have to be graceful
Otherwise I could end up remorseful.

Demanding
and
expecting
is the death
of friendship.

This week I've seen a wasp and dragonflies
Today is filled with the heat of the sun
Spring is always a tonic for the eyes
Opening my windows again is fun
It's part of my life to drive around town
I watch the metamorphosis of trees
I meditate with my car windows down
I see the world parading by at ease
The leaves of trees are unfolding again
Foliage is brightly multicolored
My movement outside is carefree again
The liveliness of earth is uncovered
There comes a point with the unfolding leaves
When I rejoice with the beauty of trees.

Suddenly
effervescent
foliage dazzles
the landscape
again.

The geese and swallows and turkey vultures
The crows and eagles and the chickadees
I see them fly and they make me wonder
What would life be like to be feathery
The quality of the wind and the air
Is common to them all but each of them
Takes to their wings with a suitable flair
And they manage the blusters as they come
I see the crows get blown off of their course
I watch the geese adapt in formations
Eagles are experts at focusing force
Vultures will soar on thermal vibrations
Swallows flicker and turn like acrobats
Chickadees are delicate acrobats.

The birds are not
separate from the
air and wind and
earth and trees
and the seasons.

I believe my cellphone is wearing out
Because I have to charge it all day long
Perhaps the battery is burning out
With a replacement I could carry on
But there are faster phones on the market
With speedier internet connections
With better attractive apps to pocket
Prompting a festival of selections
Perhaps I have forgotten my passwords
Resetting them again is a hassle
Reducing me to a frustrated nerd
Lost in a technological dazzle
I like to be hypnotized by my phone
It is much more fabulous than the moon.

I would feel
practically naked
adrift and isolated
without a functioning
cellphone.

Fingers and toes — elbows knees and ankles
I flex them each day of my existence
They do so much more than merely dangle
They offer me primary assistance
I couldn't ride a bike without my knees
Couldn't have breakfast without my elbows
With ankles I can gambol at my ease
With ankles and knees I can really flow
My fingers are most handy instruments
Futzing with a cellphone and computer
For scratching they are such good implements
I can unfasten buttons as a lover
But I'm not sure what my toes are doing
Trimming toenails is excruciating.

My fingers assist
in the trimming of
toenails but I
really have to
scrunch myself.

Dandelions are appearing again
Simultaneous with creeping charlie
Asserting themselves following the rain
Dandelions are certainly hardy
I am the only one who mows my lawn
It's my weekly responsibility
For more than twenty years I've carried on
Watching dandelion fertility
I used to think of them as nasty weeds
Their presence disturbed my tranquility
I resented the puffs that spread their seeds
But I have gained some flexibility
I don't think about what I'm stepping on
Just doing what I do — mowing the lawn.

After the puffs of seeds
dissipate in spring
the persistent yellow
flowers are cheerful.

I'm learning what to do with solitude
How do I manage thinking by myself?
All my hours are filled with my attitude
How may a person be good to oneself?
For a year I've taken to watching trees
And they don't show an inch of symmetry
These are the days of the unfolding leaves
A time of natural festivity
I especially like crabapple trees
I enjoy the color of their flowers
They bloom and leaf simultaneously
I absorb their beauty and can't be sour
Feeling optimism is a power
I turn to trees almost every hour.

Even when motionless in
the absence of a wind
the trees are weirdly
expressive.

Society is divided today
With political animosity
Even during the lovely days of May
The media conveys hostility
The pandemic virus has been awful
We have shut the schools and closed businesses
A year of sickness has been terrible
Many have died but most are witnesses
We are so suspicious of each other
That our leaders are the targets of scorn
In isolation everyone suffers
So many are too furious to mourn
And yet between my friends and family
I have the grace of a community.

Some of the leaves
are almost fully
grown while others
are only budding.

I am looking forward to normalcy
When we can go to places without masks
When we can mingle again carelessly
And then I will dump my masks in the trash
Our aimed-for goal is herd immunity
Everyone needs to be vaccinated
Shots are dispersed in each community
Soon we hope to be emancipated
The New York Times has other opinions
A writer doubts our herd immunity
Too many are making bad decisions
So we will mask up indefinitely
Too many are refusing to get shots
My stomach is tied in terrible knots.

There is suspicion
that elite leadership
doesn't want to relinquish
the power of
domination.

I practice arranging thoughts into lines
Putzing in the selection of the words
Adding the ornamentation of rhymes
While admitting that the rhyming is absurd
The lines are composed of symbols and signs
Pretending to mirror reality
As if words and reality align
And the facts and my emotions agree
The left margin is making a sideline
Always anchored with capital letters
But my exuberance isn't confined
It's getting easy to burst the fetters
Every day my intentions are the same
This poetry is a light-hearted game.

The pages are composed
of numbered Houdini tricks
with words signifying
hours of frivolity.

There is a person whom I resented
Over a question of who's dominant
Our opinions are starkly divided
And on occasion I am obstinate
We have argued at social gatherings
And afterward I considered who won
When alone I found myself arguing
The consequences of fighting weren't done
Eventually I chose to walk away
Leaving behind some people whom I like
Which has led to more solitary days
But it's better than getting into fights
And now I haven't seen him for a while
Until yesterday when he waved and smiled.

I drove ahead
with much
lingering
bitterness
dissipated.

My eyesight has always been terrible
I depend totally on my glasses
In choosing frames I am fashionable
Believing that my round frames are classics
But my lenses are chipped and breaking down
A bifocal part has become fuzzy
I went to the optometrist in town
Resigned to spend a lot of my money
And he told me about my cataracts
That it's almost time to have them removed
Afterward I won't need glasses perhaps
That my vision would be so much improved
But I'm waiting to get on Medicare
Making the expense easier to bear.

I'm used to seeing
through the smudges
And nicks of my
lenses.

I make a big deal of the blooms of spring
In poetry exaggerating in
A way that I don't do in casual
Conversation with my friends because when

Something is put on the pristine whiteness
Of a page of paper or is read to
Group of people it is an occasion
For the distillation of and for the

Celebration of the periodic
Appearance of beauty punctuating
And turning the humdrum business of life
Into something special even though I

Know that between my garage and house
Only one red tulip will be blooming.

Tulips abound
about town but
I love my single
bloom by the
garage.

I am a believer in the troughs and
Crests of life having experienced the
Intimacy and the solicitude
Of love for a time which I assumed would

Continue indefinitely and now
I know how it feels to have love withdrawn
Suddenly and seemingly without a
Reason and there's anger and hurt and a

Compulsion to figure out what happened
But really there's nothing to do but to
Receive the disorientation of
A loss which is a trough on the way to

Becoming a crest while accepting the
Traumatic quality of emotion.

Each personality
leaves ripples
merging into
incessant
undulation.

It's funny how over time a person
Gets used to the way that things appear and
I have been wearing my round glasses with
Treated lenses that turn brown in sunlight

For eight or nine years and didn't notice
When they became smudged and chipped as I am
Attending to the panorama and
Metamorphosis of the earth but now

The state of my lenses and my waiting
For Medicare eligibility
Has forced me to return to an older
Pair of glasses that are almost as good

Though not as stylish and I have to raise
My chin repeatedly to see clearly.

My neck is sore and
adjusting to new motion
as I look through the
lower half of the
bifocals.

Is it hard to imagine how life must
Have appeared to Karen Carpenter who
Was a celebrated American
Singer but who could not overcome the

Self-critical and the despairing thoughts
Coming from absorbing her image in
A mirror reflecting a consciousness
Of never being good enough leading

To a compulsion to starve herself of
Nutrition to be ever slimmer than
She was eventually bringing on
Heart failure and death — it is hard to grasp

How hypnotizing and encompassing
A vision in a mirror can become.

It is hard to imagine
how life could be
without looking
into mirrors.

On the chilly days of spring I can ride
My bicycle again after watching
It leaning against my dining room wall
For the entirety of the winter

Reminding me of my captivity
Indoors and now over the Lift Bridge of
Downtown Stillwater I thrust myself up
The long incline of the hill to Houlton

Rising off of the bicycle seat and
Dancing upright on the pedals gauging
My pacing up the hill repeatedly
Over days and weeks making the ascent

A worthy cynosure of my twenty-
Mile circuit on glorious afternoons.

My high-tech bicycle
leaning against my
dining room wall is
an eloquent vision
of arrested speed.

There are spring snow crabapple trees blooming
Around Stillwater coincident with
The unfolding of leaves and already
Some of the blossoms are scattering from

The trees in the wind spreading on the streets
And the grass looking not so much like snow
To me but like confetti left over
From a parade that has passed by and the

Pristine whiteness and the delicate and
Velvety texture of petals fallen
On the ground conveys to me a tinge of
Transience and sadness as an event

That I've looked forward to for many months
Is reaching fulfillment and is going.

My years of living
in Japan habituated
me to the celebration
and the transience
of flowering trees.

Tightly wound and pink buds are appearing
On my apple trees by the driveway and
Across the yard the lilac blossoms are
Emerging as the creeping charlie and

The dandelions are already well
Established and leaves of the towering
Cottonwood are half-grown and sparkling in
The sun and I wonder at the buds of

The apple tree that are pink and yet in
Their full expression they become white and
Every year I watch the blooming of my
Yard looking for something special to say

About these predictable events and
I guess what matters is they bring me joy.

The spring leaves
are luminous with
the sun for a while
and then they lose
their luster.

Space between the trees reverberates with
The various and persistent sounds of
The birds in the morning and the extent
Of the cloudless sky is only partly

Hinted at by the towering height of
The cottonwood at the corner of my
Yard and all the emerging leaves up and
Down the cottonwood are moving in a

Chilly breeze and flickering with the light
Of the sun giving the space between the
Tree and me through which the breeze is blowing
A sensuous and an almost liquid

Quality and words cannot do justice
But can only hint at undulation.

The space about my car
left a paper-thin layer
of ice on my windshield
that I am scraping off.

So many people I know do speak of
The love of God who sustains them in a
Gentle embrace empowering them to
Overcome difficulties and answering

For them a need of reassurance and
Of strength allaying the underlying
And the nagging of doubts that cause so much
Trouble and doubts add such poignancy to

Everyday events and I'm not so much
Different only I don't pigeonhole
God inside of a personality
Directing events but I wonder how

Everything arises from emptiness
And returns so oddly to emptiness.

I believe
degrees of suffering
are various but
consciousness is
indestructible.

The space between the things of the world that
We move and live within and from which we
Witness again the awakening and
The flourishing of spring wherein the grass

Grows and the tulips and cherry trees and
And hepatica bloom and the pussy
Willows open and the robins and killdeer and
Blue herons and redwing blackbirds and the

Grackles arrive from migration and the
Mourning cloak butterflies activate from
Hibernation this space between which the
Earth is resurrected again in spring

Is space/mind arising with sensations
Fostering experience and knowledge.

The emptiness from which
space/mind emerges is
the absence of sensation
experience and knowledge.

A girl named River who has multiple
Sclerosis and uses devices to
Help her move about assisted me for
An afternoon in the composition

Of business cards enabling me to
Better present myself as a poet
Within a circle of poets that she
Knows about because she is a worthy

Poet and an artist herself and I
Enjoyed the time conjoining paintings of
An indigo bunting and a sunburst
With colored letters and numbers and with

Rounded corners and textured paper and
I will cherish the day that we made cards.

River prepared
golden milk with
assorted spices which
we had with apples
coated with peanut butter.

The time it takes for me to choose a word
That embodies a meaning worthy of
Utterance is a kind of space — like the
Distance it takes to walk from here to there —

This kind of space has a quality that
Is measured by the things that happen and
Are remembered to have happened within
The passage of time — as can be seen when

Nothing happens and then time disappears —
But when it happens that the words come with
Ease and focused fascination then there
Is an intensity and very much

Happens in a short amount of time and
Then time may lose its semblance of order.

So perhaps time/space
is relative to what
is happening in the
moment.

Some of the leaves are almost fully grown
Other trees are only starting to bud
But is anything growing on its own?
Doesn't everything depend on a tug?
My apple trees are leafing and blooming
Without a reference to a calendar
Do they grow as they do without choosing?
Do they take their cues from the atmosphere?
I let my apple trees influence me
I planted them and have watched them growing
Through the years they are pacifying me
Apple blossom scent will soon be flowing
Apple trees and lilacs bloom together
But I don't believe that they are tethered.

It's a happy
coincidence my
lilacs on the corner
bloom with my
apple trees.

A part of me enjoys a gloomy day
When the clouds are heavy and threaten rain
When high expectations are thrust astray
Because a part of me likes to complain
I may be bad-tempered and that's OK
I am stuck at the moment and feeling strain
I can give myself a little leeway
Because elation is hard to maintain
It's good that my plans are in disarray
What is best for me I don't ascertain
I am happy to toss mistakes away
I'm just being moody — I'm not insane
I may turn my thinking without delay
Being jubilant again is child's play.

I can let the drama
drain out of my head
like air escaping
a balloon.

I waste a lot of time composing rhymes
Do you think I'm making the world better?
Poetry isn't a dreadful pastime
Cleaner than fixing a carburetor
And I try to finish before lunchtime
Afterward I work on my newsletter
No one can become a poet full time
Not without ending up as a debtor
Christopher Marlow is my paradigm
Another Elizabethan writer
But I cover the news in the meantime
I'm always looking for new subscribers
The daily news just encapsulates crime
I want a diversion from all that grime.

We have to do something
With our time —
half rhyme
eye rhyme
ragtime
pantomime.

You surely are a beautiful woman
With a delicate neck and slender shoulders
Which comport so well with ample bosoms
A striking effect on this beholder
You're posing with a careless nonchalance
Projecting unconscious self-confidence
A vision for a passion to ensconce
I savor looking without consequence
Obviously a force to contend with
A formidable conjuror of love
A risky obsession to befriend with
And once smitten so hard to dispose of
It is fetching what you do with your eyes
I don't want to believe they're telling lies.

We haven't even
spoken a word to
each other yet you've
seized my attention
with your eyes.

Do you know the word "equanimity"?
It means a person possessing balance
It is protection from fragility
Being quiet and stable is a talent
I know what it's like to be caught by love
Always desiring — living with tension
It's a trap I'm happy to be free of
It's not fun to engender suspicion
My trouble is I become possessive
Then I wonder does she really love me?
Launching thinking that becomes obsessive
I get so encumbered I can't be free
Then I start to question my dignity
My life gets tangled in perplexity.

Could I love without
engendering
possession and
suspicion?

I was given the *dharma* name "*Tekkan*"
In a ceremony involving vows
My name comes from the Zen master Dogen
His inspiration moves our Buddhist vows
He's a central figure in history
As the founder of Zen within Japan
Maybe he graces my trajectory
The name "*Tekkan*" signifies "Iron Man"
A disciple with determination
That is what my name indicates in me
I've been practicing without cessation
I do my meditation happily
But most of all I watch how I'm thinking
I aim my practice towards balanced living.

Equanimity
compassion
benevolence
altruistic joy
is the way.

Thank you — reader — for following my words
You are lending me the use of your eyes
Perhaps we are both a couple of nerds
It's a fancy game to epitomize
I would also like to borrow your heart
Maybe I could ask you to sympathize?
I turn curiosity into art
With queries and quizzes I synthesize
I'd like to explore the nature of love
Is its basic function to harmonize?
Is it also predatory? Kind of
Its primary trick is to mesmerize
To snare to burden and to tantalize
And all the while we tend to rhapsodize.

I don't want to minimize
And rather not maximize
Love is biblical
And formidable
And does tend to pulverize.

Imagine my surprise when she calls me
I was doing my work reading essays
As first she says that she's a divorcée
Which is more than a hint she wants to play
She says that her ex can be quite nasty
He expected much — she couldn't obey
Her married life was boring and messy
And she heard me speaking the other day
I seemed so intelligent and carefree
She's curious about what I have to say
She would like to get together with me
She suggested we meet and have coffee
Asking "Which are the days that I am free?"

I do distrust fantasy
I'm wary of vanity
But she is so bold
Over a threshold
Beyond rationality.

I am having trouble concentrating
The daily news has lost my interest
That phone conversation was breathtaking
And now my thinking is incoherent
I would rather not be fantasizing
I can see her tricks — I'm not ignorant
I have my essays to be editing
But I find myself a little listless
She certainly is disorienting
I could almost profess to be witless
I can see myself prevaricating
It's getting hard to focus on business
I'd like to say that this is irritating
But in my heart I know it's exciting.

She is precipitating
I am participating
Could this be love?
Coming from above?
As I am fantasizing.

She was brash to call me and I was shocked
I didn't anticipate such a move
And I was stimulated as we talked
The fact that she reached out to me is huge
She's lonely and newly separated
Desiring to know how I'm getting by
She's sad and wants to be educated
She thinks I'm cheerful and wants to know why
How is it that troubles don't get me down?
Her husband told her so many damn lies
She certain that he's been fooling around
And I'm the lucky guy who caught her eye
Suddenly my life is turned upside down
I am different but I don't know how.

I am appreciated
And now I am elated
My heart is beating
My mind is racing
I've become captivated.

This is the time of the year for lovers
The sun's bursting with energy again
So much liveliness to rediscover
And I'm feeling exuberant again
Flowering trees are at the fullest bloom
Most of the leaves are almost fully grown
Warm summer breezes are arriving soon
I may find a love that I've never known
It's so nice to be appreciated
My life has taken on a sudden turn
Which I could not have anticipated
What's coming next I really can't discern
Been a long time since I've felt so happy
I won't say more because I'll get sappy.

Now I am speculating
My heart is palpitating
And I can't sit still
As I'm feeling thrills
I am anticipating.

And now I have her number on my phone
We're meeting at Caribou for coffee
My expectations are not overblown
I intend to be a real softie
I don't remember feeling this before
A superfluity of energy
I've reached a state of opening new doors
But now my mind is wandering strangely
I'm questioning — what is she really like?
And will our conversation be easy?
I'd like to believe that we think alike
I'm getting hints that she may be teasy
She is a cutie with an easy smile
She comports herself with a sense of style.

Life is now propitious
I'm suddenly ambitious
I'm having a yen
Apart from my Zen
I'm feeling adventurous.

I am fine and I have my work to do
I have to settle and to concentrate
There are essays to edit in a queue
I need to clear my head to operate
The essays are about society
I have to correct syntax and grammar
It's important to show sobriety
Because we address serious matters
Love is very fine but now I'm busy
I just want to sit and to do my work
Can't let myself entertain a tizzy
This obsessive passion is quite a quirk
A week ago I lived differently
Considered affairs indifferently.

I like articulation
And also speculation
Want to be useful
And also truthful
I don't like agitation.

I am getting my second shot in a
Walmart about twenty miles away and
Then I'll be fully vaccinated
And immune to the pandemic virus

And free to go in most places without
Wearing a mask which has turned into a
Symbol of fear and of submission to
Bureaucratic edict which would have been

Easier to take if the mask pushers
Hadn't allowed themselves liberties that
They wouldn't allow others and so a
Threshold is passing a significant

Tension is lifting and I welcome a
Taste of anticipated normalcy.

Like dominoes
falling the stores
about town are
lifting mask
mandates.

Under the threat of impending rain I
Ride my bicycle like a greyhound in
Stride and I'm proud of myself until a
Rider comes along and passes me by

Showing me there's room for improvement and
I notice the leaves of the trees and the
Black glossy feathers of the grackles at
A high place near the bridge and next to a

Cornfield I see that the willow that serves
As a landmark is fully leaved again
And is gracefully flowing and then I
Spot a redwing blackbird fly and perch on

A slender stem of a plant that I would
Have thought was too thin to support it.

The blackbird
knows better than
I the bearing
capacity of stems.

As I am moving about I can take
A moment and gaze at the cottonwood
On my corner looking up and into
The air to see the leaves up and down the

Tree fully grown now and turning in a
Breeze which is only a slight whiff of a
Wind and I can listen to the sound of
The breeze moving the leaves and I can hear

The peaceful soothing sound of the wind in
The leaves which I haven't heard since the fall
And then I wouldn't really have noticed
Because the sighing of the leaves in the

Wind happening all summer long was a
Sound I had gotten used to and ignored.

Seeing and hearing
cottonwood leaves
wafting in a breeze
again is an interlude
in a busy day.

The second shot of the vaccine is the
One reputed to cause just a touch of
The illness and it was so with me as
I had a fever and soreness in the

Morning afterward so that I slept a
Little longer reacquainting myself
With the way the world looks from the view of
A fevered mentality resembling

A hall of funhouse mirrors reflecting
Back to me the incidents of my life
In distorted and grotesque images
Which are only mildly disturbing as

By now I know such views are only a
Trick of the mind unworthy of notice.

The world looks
very different
once I drink coffee
and get moving
again.

Rain is pounding on the roof and running
Along the gutters and the damp chilly
Air is pouring through the open windows
And rain is descending in a deluge

And the light of the morning is dimmed by
Its sudden intensity — and the view
Of pines and of the neighboring homes is
Obscured by the sheets of the falling rain —

And it's nice sheltering inside my home
Listening to the rhythmical sound of
The rain spattering on concrete seeing
The rain being absorbed into the grass

And with every inhalation of breath
My nose is filling with the smell of rain.

And just a few
moments later
the rain becomes
a gentle patter.

The media of America is
Leveraging the news and inspiring
Bitterness by demonizing people
And the schools and universities are

Aggressively ideological
Condemning historical figures and
Lawyers and judges are advocating
Political agendas apart from

The impartial application of law
And celebrity athletes and actors
Are assuming roles as political
Activists and there's a new and scary

Intolerance in America for
A genuine diversity of thought.

In American cities
violent mobs are
seizing the initiative
and taking control.

After days of rain soaking into the
Soil the grass is upthrusting and needs to
Be mowed today or it will grow enough
To clog the blades of the mower and the

Yard will be unmanageable as we
Are having hours of resplendent sun
With the drifting of scattered clouds followed
By the domination of pelting and

Spattering rain cooling the humid air
And with the returning sun birds emerge
Blue jays cardinals grackles woodpeckers
Robins and now and again I see the

Graceful flight of a single or a pair
Of sandhill cranes slicing through the moist air.

The roots of grasses
hedges and trees are
drinking water and
minerals and the leaves
are tasting sunlight.

It is a pleasantry of living that
One can arrange the letters of words on
A thin sheet of paper bound together
On the left side to form the pages of

A book in an attempt to glimpse and to
Capture the essences of life in a
Distillation of consciousness applied
To experience using syllables

And rhythm composing a language that
Hopefully performs a trick very much
Like an acrobat launched and tumbling in
The air within a millisecond poised

With flying and open hands to be grasped
And caught by a comprehending reader.

I live for moments
when the conduits of
words are left behind in
loving comprehension.

He calls me to let me know he's gotten
An accounting job and can expect a
Good salary with better benefits
And he's talkative which is a turn from

The one-word responses that he often
Gave to questions and he has friends who he
Meets with and he's prospering with his
Business degree and he wants to buy a

Condominium with a mortgage and
We share our views of the difficulties
Of politics which is a pleasure that
We understand each other and those years

When my son was troubled and beyond my
Ability to reach may be over.

Thousands of miles
away in Juneau
Alaska Joshua is
becoming
himself.

So many memories lie unsummoned
Only needing prompting to come back
To consciousness years of unhappiness
Between Yoshiko my ex-wife and I

And Joshua disharmony lasting
Almost thirty years but Joshua wants
To vacation with his mom in Japan the
Country of his birth returning her to

The home of so many complicated
Memories and what surprises me is
That Joshua on his initiative
Is intending a magnificent and

A healing gesture of reunion that
I could never have anticipated.

Joshua intends
to accompany
his mom on a
healing journey
of reunion.

I know what keeps me optimistic and
Young at heart is that I look outside of
Myself watching the intricacies of
The world and I don't have to go on a

Vacation to find reasons worthy of
Gratitude because I am calm enough
To be able to hear the sighing of
The wind in the leaves and to allow a

Swelling peacefulness come over me that
Naturally accompanies the sight
And the sound of leaves rustling in a breeze
No matter what is happening within

The human world the majesty of trees
In motion is cause for celebration.

Maybe if my thoughts are
subdued enough
I could spot a
rose-breasted grosbeak.

Hulk Hogan was a gesticulating
Good guy while Rowdy Roddy Piper was
A clever and insulting rogue and the
Undertaker was an eerie silent

Character who was benevolent and
Stone Cold Steve Austin was a working-class
Hero and Andre the Giant had a
Child-like simplicity and they were all

Operatically acrobatically
Entertaining stadiums full of fans
Bellowing body slamming and smacking
Each other with metal folding chairs and

Like the Gods of Olympus they performed
Edifying morality fables.

The World Wrestling
Entertainment show
is America's
Mount Olympus.

You keep me waiting and I am bemused
Waiting for you to get off of the phone
I am a little put off and confused
Standing awkwardly quietly alone
I'm sure you noticed that I have arrived
As I anxiously await our first date
Your sudden busyness does seem contrived
So what else am I to anticipate?
It seems you have a good sense of timing
You know how long to keep me suspended
Then you turn the mood by sweetly smiling
My budding frustration is upended
Part of me recognizes clever tricks
And part of me ignores — getting a kick.

I am excitedly
matched with a
voluptuous
temptress.

There's excitement in being overmatched
Encountering fresh and challenging games
Stimulated yes but not overwhelmed
I am not unskilled in using my brain
She's wispy slender and possesses grace
Getting divorced is difficult for her
She has such an innocent pixie face
There are lawyer expenses to incur
Her husband is now an alcoholic
How she asks do I live without boozing?
Living sober I say is a frolic
It's an unburdened life of my choosing
I am careful not to gaze at her breasts
Taking only glimpses I think is best.

She is genuinely
engaged and
interested in my
spiritual
practice.

She knows her husband isn't a nice guy
But he's been a very good provider
She's put up with his drinking and his lies
She's wanted to help but he's defied her
He is an electrical engineer
They had a large and luxurious house
Things have gotten ugly over the years
Until now he's no better than a louse
Their two grown sons have come to despise him
They are out of the house and on their own
They're exhausted and disgusted with him
The family cohesion has broken down
She's much happier living by herself
And he can drink all he wants by himself.

Her dad died early
of alcoholism and
her ex-husband's
an ugly drunk.

She knows people who have heard me speaking
She's heard I'm eloquent and effective
That I manage to live without drinking
That I'm compassionate and reflective
She wants to learn spiritual principles
And what sobriety is based upon
Her former life has made her cynical
Faith in religiosity is gone
I am in a peculiar position
A place beyond my anticipating
No longer burdened by inhibitions
Now I know my heart is palpitating
I've not been so flattered and exalted
Can't remember being so excited.

I'm supposed to be mindful
of equanimity
but such is not my
emerging
propensity.

Is this disembodied experience?
I'm becoming so infatuated
She's tantalizingly mysterious
She's passionate and yet understated
Daydreaming of her is luxurious
During the night my thoughts are excited
Losing sleep is creating weariness
I have a fear of being deflated
Perhaps she is just being curious
And her affections are calculated
Maybe I am driven by prurience
Are my possibilities limited?
Is both lusting and loving spurious?
My state of being is precarious.

Is it love or lust
that's intoxicating?
If there were medicine
would I take it?

Are such strong passions deleterious?
My serenity is dissipated
Complicating my Zen experience
But shouldn't loving be celebrated?
I'm finding my moods can be various
When doubting myself I'm devastated
Balancing feelings is precarious
Such crazy emotions are serrated
And then I find myself gregarious
Pondering her praise makes me elated
More than happy — I am delirious
I suspect I'm overstimulated
Now I am so oddly situated
But isn't love to be venerated?

In the lotus posture
a position of the
body I've practiced
more than thirty years
I must appear — serene.

To call or not to becomes a question
How to measure the weightiness of time
Her words and gestures — full of suggestions
I'm tending to business in the meantime
I am reading the daily narratives
The pressure of politics is extreme
Freighted with dishonest declaratives
The daily hypocrisy is routine
And how could I bring her to understand?
When it's taken me years to learn the game
The phony slogans are absorbed offhand
But the sound bites and truth are not the same
I do care about our society
And that may be a liability.

To the
uninitiated
making myself
understood
is difficult.

Having opinions is only human
We take possession without much thinking
I try to penetrate my delusions
To follow guidelines without much clinging
I begin each day with meditation
I watch thoughts come and let them dissipate
Part of me laughs at my own gyrations
I let my ideas proliferate
Love and politics are complicated
How could I not become a partisan?
I want results to be consummated
Propaganda may be bipartisan
Strong emotion is intoxicating
A lovely woman is hypnotizing.

A turkey vulture
warms his wings
circling in a
sunny thermal.

Infatuation comes in any season
And the brilliance of spring skies is lovely
Love has nothing to do with my reason
Watching my befuddlement is funny
I'm absorbed in love riding my bicycle
And propelled by the wind I'm riding swiftly
I am passionate — I am physical
And I am riding precipitously
Spring is awakening — with wide open skies
Now that swallows have returned to the fields
Their adroit maneuvers dazzle my eyes
They turn and dart and then suddenly wheel
I fly through the country over the ridge
Speed in the air on the Crossing Bridge.

Love is rippling
the vast river far below —
the sky is cloudless
and the river is cloudless
they are both shining blue.

Perhaps I'm being a bit of a clown
Being overly infatuated
And I'm afraid of being let down
I know what it's like to be deflated
My juices are flowing — capturing me
Something I hadn't anticipated
My obsession with her won't let me be
Nothing I'm doing is calculated
Thank God I'm not a judge or a lawyer
My rationality is compromised
I'll operate more cleverly later
Perhaps I'm being manipulated
Is she — or am I — doing this to me?
Is this a heaven? Or catastrophe?

My dear — you should see
me poised within the lotus
posture appearing
serenely composed within
such passionate vibrations.

Why would someone choose a nasty husband?
She did say that he's a good provider
She is clever and doesn't get flustered
She may be attracted to aggressors
And then why is she attracted to me?
She is intelligent and so am I
She wants to learn something from me maybe
And so I wonder what that signifies
I'm all about being poised and open
She knows that I'm seeking liberation
Some of us hit bottom and are broken
There's a saving grace in desperation
To do meditation isn't easy
This girl is coquettish and she's teasy.

A part of me knows
that I want to be needed
to be desired
by the opposite sex and
now I'm hungering again.

There's a paradox in liberation
At least of the type that I am seeking
Trying too hard creates separation
I'd like to give up the habit of grasping
There is the initial desperation
A lingering period of suffering
That's enough to inspire frustration
That culminates in a new beginning
From there what's needed is relaxation
A peace apart from unending striving
Fascination with subtle vibrations
There is patience to be cultivating
I want to surf with my motivations
I would like to balance with emanations.

Romantic love and
political victory
may be delusions
to be grasped only for a
moment before they dissolve.

A violin is tuned exquisitely
And then the music is quite eloquent
I don't put much faith in passivity
Believing right effort is relevant
I'd like to act with sensitivity
So is playing politics negligent?
It should be done with selectivity
My motives need to be benevolent
But can I keep my objectivity?
Or could I myself be malevolent?
There's confusion in relativity
Opponents are commonly arrogant
I need my strength and flexibility
I'd like to keep a sense of etiquette
But being passive is a detriment.

There could be peace in
doing my best and leaving
the results up to
cosmic vibrations beyond
anyone's permanent grasp.

The birds are noisy before the sunrise
Just listening is intoxicating
Their joyful persistence does hypnotize
But in truth the males are advertising
They are using voices to lionize
Each of the males is fiercely competing
When conniving for mates they dramatize
The allure of females must be enticing
Is my loving a lusting in disguise?
Even so is that disqualifying?
Are my motives getting crosswise?
Don't want to stop my anticipating
And I don't want to overanalyze
My newfound romance is energizing.

It's necessary
for a mommy and daddy
buddha to combine
before a baby buddha
can properly manifest.

A good part of me is leery of love
I don't want to be intoxicated
An obsession is hard to get rid of
Sooner or later I'll be deflated
I can go to the park and watch the sky
I will slow my mind and listen to birds
In the distance I can see a crane fly
And I'm not wasting any time on words
The birds will come and then the birds will go
The clouds and sun are constantly moving
The breeze in the trees does ebb and flow
The rabbits and the squirrels are scampering
My adoration becomes a plaything
I'm not hearing or seeing anything.

My obsession with
her overlays the breeze
in the trees — and the
crane flying — I don't see when
the crane is disappearing.

I haven't lived so long without seeing
That people get crazy involved in love
It's quite common to be fantasying
Of fitting together like hand in glove
But there is a certain reality
That one partner will become dominant
That one possesses the lock and the key
When the passion becomes less prominent
There has to be compatibility
And a forgoing of competition
There's hard work in responsibility
We would need a worthy compensation
When the romantic feeling drains away
We would live with each other every day.

It takes a while for
a real person to emerge
out from under the
fantasy and then how would
reality manifest?

The breeze in the leaves is inspiring
As the clouds are sometimes dimming the light
Simple observation is reviving
The clouds have dispersed and the sky is bright
I'm not really unhappy on my own
What I do with my time I can decide
I'm not going to be using my phone
I'm going to let this relationship slide
The vibrant sky is glorious today
I am watching as the birds come and go
I am happy this Memorial Day
No one is working and I can go slow
I can play with words and think as I please
And I don't have to let myself be teased.

I don't even know
whether her interest in me
goes beyond idle
curiosity and is
only a passing fancy.

The early sonneteers wrote about love
I've followed tradition and played my part
Is my emotion genuine? Sort of
But over the years I've guarded my heart
Love is worthy — love is necessary
Without loving we wouldn't populate
But I wonder what is best for Barry
Love takes more push than I can generate
This afternoon I'll ride my bicycle
The weather is going to be glorious
Looking forward makes me excitable
Pedaling freely is luxurious
For several days I've played Romeo
But my part was only a cameo.

The peonies are
budding with their glorious
superfluity
of lushness as their heavy
blossoms are bending their stems.

One of the ways to mark the progress of
The seasons for me is to come to my
Desk and to note how high the sun is in
The morning and in June there are mornings

When the room is illuminated and
I wear a straw hat with a wide brim to
Shield my eyes so that I can see the screen and
Compose addled poetry and there is

Also the day at the grocery store
When I see in the produce area
The widest bin which I recognize can
Only mean that the watermelons have

Arrived which gives me a treat after I
Ride my bicycle in the afternoon.

I can do without
the political produce
of California
but it's a happy day when
the watermelons arrive.

Every now and then on the news the word
With images will come of an earthquake
In Pakistan or rural China in
Which the concrete buildings crumble and

Crush the people left inside implying
The peril of those trapped and lingering
Buried in the massive rubble injured
And starving waiting for rescue and I

Watch the news knowing that while I brush my
Teeth in a remote location there is
Catastrophe at the neighborhood school
In the ordinary course of a day

It's hard to digest the reality
That such events are inevitable.

That death comes is
is not the difficulty
but that it comes with
such agonizing force is
fathomless perplexity.

It takes me leg-pumping effort to reach
The highest elevation across the
River on my bicycle and I note
The landmarks on the way and more likely

Than not when ascending the final slope
I see a single stem aspiring to
Be a tree and perching on that stem there
Is a redwing blackbird who notices

Me and every time I pass it chirps once
And flies away and now I expect to
See that bird on that stem recognizing
As I do that we are both creatures of

Habit with me following my circuit
And the bird viewing the world from that stem.

The redwing blackbird
possesses the stem
with a view of a hill
and a field of soybeans.

The air is a theater of action
In June as cottonwood puffs are floating
And demonstrating the buoyancy of
Air and on a long ascending slope on

The way to the Crossing Bridge there is
A swarm of gnats forcing me to tighten
My lips and narrow my eyelids lest I
Be irritated and I am spotting white

And yellow moths fluttering revealing
Their leveraging locomotion and
I have measured my speed with the eerie
Maneuverings of brilliant dragonflies

And I have followed the startled flight of
Numerous birds who weren't expecting me.

Way up
turkey vultures
eagles
glide in
thermals
of air.

The intensity of the brilliant light
Of June is worthy of celebration
As I'm facing the window absorbing
Photons that have collided together

For millions of years before reaching the
Surface of the sun liberated and
Launched as I close my eyes and notice the
Red intensity of the light and feel

The pressure of heat on my face and arms
Coincident with the pulsation of
Blood and the rhythm of my breath and I
Didn't do anything to deserve the

Sensations of life as they are a gift
And marvel worthy of celebration.

It's a natural
progression from the workings
of the sun to the
the breathing of the lungs
and the beating of the heart.

The sky absorbs the violence of a
Jackhammer and dissipates it over
Distance and while sitting in Pioneer
Park overlooking a wide river and

A winding valley southward within the
Vast distance there is always a crow a
Crane or a goose flying and there is
So very much to be seeing and I

Tend not to notice the appearance
Or disappearance of birds and only
Watch them momentarily along with
The ephemeral movement of the clouds and

The ruffling of wind in leaves and the play
Of light and shadow moving on the ground.

I'm not so
intoxicated
with people
as to be blind to
the vast horizon.

It's peculiar that people around
The world entertain an obsession
To conquer the height of Mount Everest
Relying on specialized equipment

Gradually acclimating to the
Tipsy altitudes at base camps risking
Hypoxia ascending in a crazed
Push encountering the death zone with

The starvation of oxygen to the
Brain and lungs and every cell staggering
To summit the ultimate top of the
Planet lingering precariously and

Descending to safety amid the rocks
The snow the winds and the severest cold.

The mountain is
littered with the bodies
of those who thought
the attempt was worth
the risk.

You do know how to take me by surprise
To call me in the middle of the day
You know that you're a delight for my eyes
To dangle yourself so that I obey
I had thought it better to let you go
I don't want the bother of obsession
And I am hesitant — but even so
A part of me longs to take possession
To be the body that takes your body
Of this I'm sure that you're well aware of
With all the passion that I embody
You're coaxing it forth and hinting at love
You are an unscrupulous seductress
Seizing my attention with directness.

You know enough of
my schedule to take the
opportunity
to catch me off my guard and
dazzle me with inducements.

I know you're playing on my sympathy
Praising my receptive intelligence
Relying on my ready empathy
You're expressing yourself with eloquence
You would like me to come and meet with you
You want to know how I live so simply
Won't I come to appraise what we could do?
You are confused and feeling dreadfully
How does one learn to let go of trouble?
You would like me to instruct you — you say
I can see that you're brash and quite subtle
I'd really like to come to you today
But I have chores that I have got to do
So much rigmarole to muddle through.

I know instantly
correcting and editing
syntax and grammar
hunting for hidden typos
will now be more difficult.

You want to know how not to be angry
To rise above your ex's pettiness
To not be fuming — to not be cranky
To escape the feeling of emptiness
Your daddy died of alcoholism
Your ex is a terrible drinker too
Both had narcissistic egoism
Which you ignored but really knew was true
You work during the day as a waitress
You're a happy conversationalist
And people are clueless of your distress
But the urge to chatter you can't resist
Men at work are always hitting on you
They press their luck to see what they can do.

Both your ex and your
daddy used intelligence
to be successful
providing opulent homes
in sumptuous neighborhoods.

There is some cruelty in your husband
He is disparaging and calls you names
Which is what you can no longer withstand
In response you do exactly the same
To be cutting in your comments offhand
It's easy to be critical and blame
Usually to gain the upper hand
It becomes a habit that's hard to tame
In divorce you are advancing demands
And now it's a nasty lawyering game
The goal is to gain a judge's command
There is property to righteously claim
For marriage to end like this is a shame
You are resisting an impulse to maim.

He can keep the house
in the swanky neighborhood
but he's got to sell
the boat and pay every month
a hefty spousal support.

There's more drama here than I am used to
My divorce went without complexity
Such bitterness we didn't resort to
I don't see my ex as an enemy
I guess such wild passion becomes a stew
And perhaps it's mixed up with jealousy
With so much history to muddle through
With battles continuing endlessly
And what on earth am I supposed to do
With emotion expressed desperately?
And what trouble am I getting into?
He is arrogant — she is comely
She is beautiful and he has money
He is dogmatic and she is plucky.

Were they made for each other?
To battle with one another?
To squabble and fight
Trading words that bite
Passionately together?

Not getting angry isn't so easy
I had to give up my way of thinking
To let go of victim mentality
And to stop my alcoholic drinking
You can't make a change temporarily
How does one do it without backsliding?
I had to be crushed fundamentally
Such experience isn't appealing
Hitting bottom is a necessity
Otherwise any progress is fleeting
Now I practice in a community
Communication is empowering
I need new power to grow into
A power to give my frustrations to.

The practice becomes
"Let go or be dragged."

Apparently there are some painful pleasures
Where couples come to trouble each other
Subjecting themselves to endless pressure
Jealously squabbling with one another
I wonder what she is seeing in me
Attending and speaking so carefully
Carelessly placing her hand on my knee
Moving in closely quite casually
I know what's happening — I really do
As I notice her eyes are powder blue
Such an intoxicating point of view
I will see what she wants and muddle through
Her fetching presence is tantalizing
Her voice and her words are hypnotizing.

Her curves are tantalizing
Her voice is hypnotizing
But I am careful
And I'm respectful
While she is appetizing.

You know I'm captivated by your charms
And that being with you makes me happy
How could conversing come to any harm?
We are both so fluent and word-savvy
It's not necessary to squabble and fight
I have learned how to live quite peacefully
I don't have trouble sleeping overnight
I've avoided worry successfully
The tricks of detachment I can show you
How to absorb the sunlight — how to breathe
The peace of the *dharma* I can give you
I could navigate with you if you please
You could let go of all your agitation
We could enlighten your cogitation.

Your ex knows how to
manipulate to coerce
you and to push your
buttons befuddling and
destroying your happiness.

The mind operates precariously
What we think about we give power to
Our thoughts happen so precipitously
What we think about we give ourselves to
I have governed myself deceitfully
Supposing I'm controlling what I do
Passion with peace exists uneasily
Sometimes my emotions are torn in two
I aspire to live and love gracefully
And you are showing me that you do too
To think and behave harmoniously
I'm happy to get together with you
To express and to listen equally
I've not had satisfaction recently.

I'm wondering how
such a lovely woman as
yourself could be so
taken in with a person
so unsuited to yourself?

"I was captured by his virility" —
She says — "by his aggression and his looks
His professional capability
Though I knew he was a bit of a crook
But now his behavior has gotten worse
Becoming no more than a drunken louse
There's a quality to him that's perverse
He'd rather have me shut inside the house
I see you operate differently
That you're authentically compassionate
Which is kind of rare — incidentally
And that your words are strangely resonant
I am coming to see that intelligence
Expresses an attractive elegance.

"I don't think you know
the influence of your words
I am curious
how it is you became so
intuitive?" she asks me.

I'm walking about in a happy daze
So satisfied and anticipating
My daydreaming has been a little crazed
Experience is intoxicating
And my meditation is going well
Sitting not moving for forty minutes
Absolutely no problem sitting still
I practice to keep cerebral fitness
I'm doing my editing well enough
Sometimes I am losing my train of thought
Philosophical stuff is kind of tough
Doing the business is an afterthought
In truth I'm reliving my night with her
Ordinary activities are blurred.

I am a nerd who
astonishingly caught a
delightful fish and
now the world is appearing
surprisingly different.

I'm really confused and somewhat put off
So why isn't she answering my calls?
It appears suddenly she's cut me off
Didn't expect to encounter a wall
I do remember reminding myself
Intoxication ends in depression
My sad situation speaks for itself
I guess I'm not done with learning lessons
I've got to decide what I'm going to do
I imagine myself being resolute
Maybe I did something — made a miscue?
Can't stop thinking about her attributes
I'm not going to fret — I'm not going to call
I'm not going to do anything at all.

The Chinese poet
Cold Mountain left the city
kicked off the red dirt
of civilization and
lived with mountains and rivers.

Within two weeks of June the white roses
With a tinge of pink on my patio
And the lushly pink peonies in my
Yard are blooming as the blaze of the

Sun is strengthening as the seasonal
Orbit of the earth about the sun is
Approaching the point of summer solstice
Extending the length of daylight to its

Apogee as roses and peonies
Coincide at my humble abode with
The direction of the solar system
And it happens that the ritual of

My noticing this happy occurrence
Is worthy of quiet celebration.

The cottonwood on
the corner of my yard
is deploying its
array of fully unfolded
leaves absorbing the sunlight.

In a week of afternoons of 90-
Degree Fahrenheit heat I am every
Day ascending the furthest slope with the
Highest elevation of my circuit

On my bicycle on the lookout for
The chirping redwing blackbird who has been
Perching habitually on a stem
And I'm noticing its absence as it's

Apparent that the blaze of the sun is
Too much for the bird and I agree as
I couldn't bear sitting in this shadeless
Heat either but I also notice the

Three-foot stem by the road is a baby
Cottonwood displaying distinctive leaves.

How many of the
numerous aspiring
baby cottonwoods
so clustered together will
escape the county mower?

On a cloudless morning at Pioneer
Park during our gathering while we are
Lounging within lawn chairs discussing a
Way of living apart from addictions

Fran is informing me of the warblers
She is hearing the red-eyed vireo
Olive green above and clean white below
With tail feathers of a green-yellow wash

And the American redstart the males
Black with orange patches and the females
Gray and olive with yellow patches — and
The birds are invisible concealed by

Foliage but their singing is lively
And punctuating our conversation.

Beyond addictions
there are invisible song
birds to be on the
lookout for brightening an
otherwise bland existence.

My thoughts are whirling in captivity
I can't help wondering what you're doing
I feel the lure of compulsivity
As my mind is busy speculating
I am confused within uncertainty
Weighing each of our words — analyzing
Do you control me surreptitiously?
Your motivations are mystifying
I did enjoy you unabashedly
Now your sudden absence is perplexing
What's with this unavailability?
My ignorance is disorienting
Don't know why you're not returning my calls
Suddenly you've erected a brick wall.

My ignorance and
confusion manifests in
scenarios on
top of scenarios that
only inspire longing.

You are a shadow companion to me
Everywhere I go I'm thinking of you
We had such an engaging repartee
Not many women banter as you do
Your words your beauty come along with me
You're an added dimension in my head
I've become a Romeo wannabe
I did have a hint of trouble ahead
I think I'm in love with being in love
I'm using you to hypnotize myself
It's the idea of loving I love
I'm pulling a mighty trick on myself
I'm stuck right now and don't know what to do
My head is busy imagining you.

Infatuation
is a gas transporting me
into whimsical
departures destinations
of happy permutations.

I don't have to be encumbered with you
Comport yourself exactly as you please
You are much more controlling than I knew
You are a voluptuous tricky tease
I am going to go about my business
I have many important things to do
Love is disorienting dizziness
There's more to do than to think about you
I do have my bicycle and my cat
And I can look at my cottonwood tree
You are no more trouble than summer gnats
You are not getting me to bend a knee
Our meeting wasn't serendipity
You've only taken my serenity.

I do want liberation
I enjoyed our flirtation
I not going to fret
Do you want to bet?
I don't want a fixation.

The sun has been burning so brilliantly
The roots of the growing grass are busy
There's no reason to mope despondently
To befuddle myself and become lazy
I just bought a bicycle computer
I can track my time and average speed
To discipline myself and go faster
It takes method and practice to succeed
Where you are doesn't matter much to me
I've got plenty to occupy my time
And what you're doing doesn't concern me
I think maybe I will compose some rhymes
I'm perfectly free to do as I please
Why should I bother with ticks gnats and fleas?

The world is still rotating
The hardy grass is growing
There are things to do
And places to go
There's no need to be moping.

You won't return my calls — I don't know why
I don't think I can do anything more
Probably it's better to say goodbye
It is beyond me to open your door
From now on I know what has to be done
I need to upend and guard my thinking
The excitement I felt can't be undone
You are even disturbing my sleeping
I have to stop when thinking about you
And instantly think about something else
I've got to come up with tricks that will do
I want to think about anything else
Perhaps I can tinker with poetry
And turn my attention to clarity.

Words are always enticing
Composing is inviting
I don't have to lie
I look at the sky
Dragonflies are beguiling.

So differently from my phone which dazzles
My eyes with gaudy and harsh vibrations
When I gaze at the immensity of
Of the sky filled with the ephemeral

And the soothing quality of the clouds
Moving so gradually that one must
Watch attentively and calmly to see
Motion I know that I can dissipate

Disturbance with simple observation
And today amid the towering clouds
I am catching sight of the tiniest
Silhouette of a bird so high up that

I wonder what it's doing so far above
The earth and then it dissolves in the air.

Clouds do express
such ephemeral landscapes
shadowy valleys
and sunlit mountainous peaks
slowly metamorphizing.

In Pioneer Park while leaning back in
My lawn chair and noticing the fully
Grown maple and oak leaves that have now lost
Their sheen of spring brightness I also see

At the edge of my short pants and at the
Ends of the sleeves of my T-shirt there is
A demarcation visible between
The palest of my skin untouched by the

Rays of the sun and a new eminence
Of browning skin which is a token of
The energy of sunlight gracing my
Body during my bicycle rides

About the ups and downs of the river
Valley — and I feel exhilarated.

I imagine my
body as a marshmallow
browning in the fire
of effervescent sunlight
approaching its peak brilliance.

Once the scorching temps relent and summer
Heat returns to milder degrees there are
Cooler interludes in the morning when
The air is suffused and saturated

With the brilliant light of the season and
It's a pleasure to close my eyes facing
The sun and to immerse my consciousness
Within the flushed radiance about my

Face and to see the red quality
Of the light filtered by my eyelids
And I realize that I have waited
A very long time for the pleasures of

Summer to return — to be at my ease
Cavorting in skimpy shorts and T-shirts.

To enjoy the scent
of the white roses on my
patio I have
to immerse my nose in the
petals and inhale deeply.

They aren't as classically beautiful as
The roses but the innumerable
Blooms of white clover are here replacing
The flowering of the dandelions

And creeping charlie and I see monarch
Butterflies and the yellow and white moths
And the dragonflies and fruit flies and
The bumblebees as the permutations

Of summer are coming about again
And I don't mind doing the chores of the
Yard pacing behind the mower once a
Week around the patio apple

Trees the lilac bushes the cottonwood
And I finish in front beside the two pines.

The glare of the sun
is arduous on the hill
and I look forward
to the shady cottonwood
on the northwest corner.

I remember
a woman's
powder blue eyes
and her hand
on my knee.

—*Tekkan*

www.ingramcontent.com/pod-product-compliance
Lightning Source LLC
Chambersburg PA
CBHW040421100526
44589CB00021B/2784